game night
PARTIES

Planning a *Bash* that Makes Your
Friends Say "Yeah!"

by Jen Jones

CAPSTONE PRESS
a capstone imprint

Snap Books are published by Capstone Press,
1710 Roe Crest Drive, North Mankato, Minnesota 56003
www.capstonepub.com

Library of Congress Cataloging-in-Publication Data
Jones, Jen.
  Game night parties : planning a bash that makes your friends say "yeah!" / by Jen Jones.
    pages cm. — (Snap books. Perfect parties.)
  Summary: "Learn how to throw a game-night bash that will go down in history. Discover themes, decorations, food, and planning tips that will kick off the perfect party"-- Provided by publisher.
  ISBN 978-1-4765-4006-1 (library binding)
  ISBN 978-1-4765-6053-3 (eBook PDF)
1. Children's parties—Planning—Juvenile literature. 2. Games—Juvenile literature. I. Title.

GV1205.J646 2014
793.2'1—dc23   2013043392

Editorial Credits
Mari Bolte, editor; Tracy Davies McCabe, designer; Kathy McColley, production specialist;
Sarah Schuete, photo stylist; Sarah Schuette and Marcy Morin, project creators

Photo Credits
Photography by Capstone Studio: Karon Dubke except: Shutterstock: aboikis, 13 (bottom), Africa Studio, 22, Brian Goodman, 13 (middle bottom), Elaine Barker, cover (top), 1, Filip Fuxa, 12 (bottom), Gemenacom, 16 (bottom), Goran Bogicevic, 19, Iakov Filimonov, 15 (right), Ildi Papp, 16 (top), JMiks, 11 (front), Joana Lopes, 31 (bottom), Käfer photo, 19 (inset), Kamenetskiy Konstantin, 31 (top), Lucky Business, 15 (top), Magdalena Kucova, 6 (top), Mandy Godbehear, 11 (back), Mariontxa, 23, Monkey Business Images, 14 (top), Olivier Le Queinec, 18 (top), Philip Stridh, 13 (middle top), prudkov, 15 (bottom), racom, 30, Rob Marmion, 14 (bottom), Robyn Mackenzie, 12 (middle), Ruth Black, 27, Stephen Rees, 12 (top), Tatiana Popova, 12 (right), Teresa Kasprzycka, 13 (top), violetblue, 14 (middle)

Design Elements:
Shutterstock: andersphoto, Jack Jelly, Petrosg, qvist, Yganko

Printed in the United States of America in Brainerd, Minnesota.
092013   007770BANGS14

TABLE OF CONTENTS

Getting Started

It's not hard to see why people love parties so much. After all, they're festive, fun, and celebrate something that's really important—friendship. The best hostesses throw parties that bring new people together. That's where you come in!

The trick is planning a party that your friends won't forget. Creativity is the key—any interest or hobby can be transformed into a party theme. Get inspired with two unforgettable party ideas. You've Got Game will put you in first place as the #1 hostess. Movie Under the Stars will have them star-struck over your party-planning skills. First, pick your theme. Then find oodles of ideas for making your party pop!

Of course, it's true that a hostess' work is never done. Endless to-do lists and lots of hands-on tasks often translate to lots of hard work for a hostess. Luckily, it can be a lot of fun—and a lot easier with the right insider intel! The right info can keep you organized, savvy, and sane as you plan your big shindig. Learn ways to cover all of the bases while preparing for your party—and hit a home run with the result.

YOU'VE GOT GAME

Here's a real winner—a mystery box game night. No need to roll the dice on whether your guests will have fun. This party is a sure bet!

In-Style Invite

Forget the Queen of Hearts. You'll be the queen of invites with this deck of cards. Print out the party info onto brightly colored cardstock. Then glue the info onto the back of a giant playing card.

Setting the Stage

Since you'll be sitting around a table, why not use a nifty nameplate? Mark each person's spot with a personalized name tag. Stick to the theme and use Scrabble tiles to spell out each name. You can also use this trick for labeling eats and treats at the food table.

Deck the walls with lots of game boards! From Monopoly to Life, board games make awesome wall hangings. And the creativity doesn't stop there–what about using a Twister mat as a tablecloth? For a dessert table centerpiece, pay tribute to Go Fish with a festive fishbowl.

Would your friends do anything for money? There's only one way to find out! As they arrive, hand each person $200 in Monopoly money. During the party, people can bribe each other to do silly things in exchange for dough. Whoever has the most moolah at the end gets a prize!

Eats and Treats

Set up a "Candy Crush Corner." Fill mason jars with treats such as hard candies, gumdrops, and swirly lollipops. Let your friends "combine" candies by bagging their favorites for later.

YOU'VE GOT GAME

Popular Indoor Games:

SCENE IT!
MONOPOLY
CLUE
CATCHPHRASE
TABOO
SCATTERGORIES

Awesome Outdoor Games:

BEANBAG TOSS
LADDER GOLF
BOCCE
THREE-LEGGED RACE
WATER BALLOON PINATA
FRISBEE GOLF
LAWN TWISTER

Take indoor games outside! Make life-sized versions of these classic games. Use balls, balloons, boxes, Frisbees, and large pieces of cardboard to recreate game pieces.

DON'T BREAK THE ICE
PING-PONG
JENGA
PICTIONARY

HI HO CHERRY-O
CONNECT FOUR
BANANAGRAMS

Signature Sip: Apples to Apples

Be the apple of everyone's eye with this sparkling signature sip!

- 1 bottle sparkling apple cider
- 1 cup (240 mL) cranberry juice
- ½ cup (120 mL) orange juice

Stir all ingredients together, and serve. Use red and green cups topped with brown straws to really pull the theme together.

Favors with Flavor:

- Mad Libs books
- fuzzy dice
- deck of cards

MOVIE UNDER THE STARS

Lights, camera, action! A backyard movie night is the perfect excuse to spread out under the stars. Grab a blanket, and watch a classic in the company of your real-life co-stars.

THE SET-UP

Bringing the big screen to your shindig isn't as hard as you might think. Don't spend money on an outdoor movie screen. Instead, use a wall or tie a large white sheet to two trees or poles. You'll also need a portable DVD projector to show the flick on your screen of choice. For seating, set up a bunch of comfy blankets, beanbags, or lawn chairs. Finally, light some citronella candles to keep the bugs at bay!

Setting the Stage

With this party, timing is everything! You'll want to start the movie as soon as it gets dark, so invite everyone to arrive just before dusk. That will provide plenty of time for chatting, noshing, and getting cozy before the big flick.

Make your party pop-ular! Set up a popcorn bar with tons of trimmings and toppings. Offer staples like kettle corn, white cheddar popcorn, and classic butter. For those with truly daring taste buds, set out plain popcorn and an array of toppings. Test out dry ranch powder, caramel syrup, or spicy sriracha sauce.

Go the extra mile with props like movie reels, a production slate, and striped popcorn boxes. Create a "Walk of Fame" down your driveway using large stars with your friends' names on them.

In-Style Invite

That's the ticket! Pass out an adorable invite in the style of an "Admit One" movie stub! Make your own or browse the many styles available online.

Eats and Treats

Along with the popcorn bar, consider setting up a concession stand for traditional faves like licorice, candy bars, and nuts. Choose soft pretzels and hot dogs for more filling treats.

Now Showing—The Classics

If you've seen all the latest flicks and are looking for something classic, stop here! Some can't-miss girlfriend picks include:

- *Breakfast at Tiffany's* (1961)
- *Casablanca* (1942)
- *National Velvet* (1944)
- *Clueless* (1995)
- *Grease* (1978)
- *Singin' in the Rain* (1952)
- *Gone With The Wind* (1939)
- *Some Like It Hot* (1959)
- *West Side Story* (1961)
- *Say Anything …* (1989)
- *A League Of Their Own* (1992)
- *10 Things I Hate About You* (1999)
- *Pitch Perfect* (2012)

Favors with Flair:

- popcorn balls
- big sunglasses and feather boas
- mini trophies that look like Oscars

Signature Sip: Cola Queen

Go classic Hollywood with a Roy Rogers or a Shirley Temple—but add a limey twist! These soda-based sips put a fun spin on this classic movie beverage.

- 1 tablespoon (15 mL) grenadine
- 1 tablespoon (15 mL) lime juice
- 1 can of soda (cola for a Roy Rogers, lemon-lime for a Shirley Temple)

Combine all ingredients in a tall glass and enjoy! For extra flair, add star-shaped straw toppers or crushed ice.

YOU'VE GOT GAME

Movie trivia time – test your besties on just how well they know their fave flicks. Whoever gets the most correct answers snags a pair of movie tickets or a DVD!

You're Invited

The two words everyone loves to hear—You're invited! Invites are an awesome way to get people excited for your party. They also set the tone for what's to come. Tying the invite to the party theme gets the fun started long before the party begins.

You've Got Mail

There are two main ways to send invites—e-mail and snail mail. Both have benefits. E-mail is quick and easy. Snail mail makes guests feel special and often allows for more creativity. The good news? There's no wrong way to do it! If you decide to go the e-mail route, check out invitation websites for fun and fab design options.

One tip—if you send invites over the Internet, check your privacy settings! Make sure guests can't share or forward their invites, or you might end up with lots of extra attendees.

Don't-Miss Details

Wondering what info to include? Use this handy-dandy rundown:

- your name
- party occasion or theme
- brief description of the party
- day, date, and time
- location and address
- R.S.V.P. date and contact info
- suggested dress code (if necessary)

'80s PARTY

Mackenzie's '80s-Tastic Birthday Bash!
Hosted By Mackenzie Martin

Girls just wanna have fun! Bust out your best neon and big hair!
Let's travel back in time together to the totally awesome '80s.

When:
Saturday, August 2nd
1:00 p.m. – 4:00 p.m.

Where:
Mackenzie's Time Machine
123 Main Street

Please R.S.V.P. no later than July 27th by emailing
mackenzie@emailvites.com or calling 555-xxx-xxxx.

Your Party Style

What's your party décor personality?
Take this quick quiz to find out:

You're at the party supply store. What catches your eye?

a) a brightly colored vase

b) a cool old chalkboard

c) a picnic basket with plaid trim

d) an oversized peacock feather centerpiece

Who's your style icon?

a) Taylor Swift

b) Zooey Deschanel

c) Rachel Bilson

d) Demi Lovato

Your dream dinner party would be:

a) a modern around-the-world feast

b) a communal dinner in a cool barn

c) a lively backyard barbecue

d) an eight-course extravaganza

If you answered mostly A, you're **Bold and Bright**

If you answered mostly B, you're a **Classic Cutie**

If you answered mostly C, you're a **Down-Home Darling**

If you answered mostly D, you're a **Drama Queen** (in the best way, of course!)

De-Stress R/x

Just hours away from the party, you're feeling anything but calm, cool, and collected. Sound familiar? You're not alone—lots of party planners feel frazzled right before things get going. Avoid having a hostess meltdown by following a few simple rules.

Beat the rush. If you think party prep will take three hours, make it four! Prep work always takes longer than expected, and starting early will guarantee plenty of time to deal with any pesky last-minute probs.

Pump up the volume. Get into the party spirit before guests arrive by turning on some tunes! Listening to music as you get ready will make it more fun and melt away the stress.

Phone a friend. Why do everything solo when you can harness the power of two? It's practically in the BFF contract that your bestie will be there to help you when you need it. Enlist a friend to come early and help you and your family whip everything into shape.

Leave time for looking great.
Lots of hostesses get stuck rushing around and end up barely dressed when the party starts. Don't be that girl! When figuring out your prep time, work in an hour for getting pretty. Take time for a relaxing shower and to primp properly. This extra time will help you look good—and feel great—in your party outfit by the time the guests arrive.

Par-tay! (It's Finally Time)

The clock is ticking. In just a short time, your guests will be walking through that front door. Will you be ready? Use this checklist to keep your day-of-party prep on track.

☐ Eat something. A hostess running on empty is a recipe for disaster! Eat foods that will fill you up now and give you energy for later. Fruits and veggies are always good choices. Add a handful of pumpkin seeds and a square or two of dark chocolate, and you'll be fueled up by party time.

☐ Do a final clean sweep a few hours before the party begins. Clear any clutter, dust or wipe down any surfaces that need it, and give rooms one final vacuum.

☐ You've probably completed most of the cooking over the last few days. Now is the time to finish prepping and presenting your food! Ask your parents to help you complete any kitchen tasks that still need to happen before guests arrive.

☐ If need be, make a quick run to the store for any emergency needs or things you may have forgotten. Even better—send a family member with a list. That will give you more time to prep.

☐ All of your hard work is about to get the spotlight. If you haven't already, set up any last-minute decorations.

Kitchen Confidential

Not quite a domestic diva just yet? Not to worry! No one expects you to transform overnight. Easy recipes can be just as tasty as expert ones. Here's what you need to know to conquer the kitchen with ease:

Organize and clean out the fridge to make room for all the new groceries. Pitch anything that's past its prime.

Try to choose recipes that use some of the same ingredients. It will simplify both shopping and cooking.

If possible, do a "dry run" of any new recipes before the party. Knowing how the recipes work (and taste) will come in handy. You'll also gain more kitchen confidence for the big day.

Know how you'll keep foods at their proper temp during the party. Hot foods should be kept at least 140 degrees Fahrenheit (60 degrees Celsius). Keep hot food safe by using chafing dishes, slow cookers, or warming trays. Cold foods should be kept at 40°F (4°C) or below. Keep things cool by using ice-filled nesting dishes.

Outlook: Good

Today's fortune: "You will make an amazingly easy yet tasty recipe." Whether you serve these at a glitzy game night or a fun film festival, these fortune cookies are winners.

- small strips of paper
- cookie decorating marker
- hand mixer
- 2 egg whites
- ¼ cup (60 mL) white sugar

- 4 tablespoons (60 mL) butter, melted
- ½ cup (120 mL) flour, sifted
- ¼ teaspoon (1.2 mL) vanilla extract
- baking sheet
- parchment paper

1. Write fun fortunes on small strips of paper with a cookie decorating marker.

2. Use a hand mixer to whip egg whites until they're foamy.

3. Add sugar. Continue to mix until soft peaks form.

4. Add butter, flour, and vanilla. Mix until combined.

5. Drop a tablespoon of batter onto a baking sheet lined with parchment. Use the spoon to spread the batter in an even circle. Bake only a few cookies at a time.

6. Bake at 350°F (180°C) for six to eight minutes.

7. When cookies are golden, remove from the baking sheet with a spatula and place on cool surface. Place a fortune onto each cookie.

8. Work quickly to fold cookie in half over the fortune. Then bend the cookie over the edge of the spatula to form a crescent.

Other Ideas

- To give your cookies a bright burst, color the batter with food coloring before baking. Drop dots of colored batter onto uncolored batter rounds to create patterns.

- Use extracts to make orange, lemon, coconut, or other flavored cookies. Add a 1-ounce (30-gram) square of melted baking chocolate for chocolate cookies.

- Surprise your guests with a shower of color! Add edible pearls, large sprinkles, or confetti before you fold the fortune cookie in half.

- Pipe decorations onto cookies with melted candy coating and a piping bag.

- Dip one half in chocolate and the other half in white chocolate for yin-yang cookies.

- Make giant cookies! Make the dough balls as large as you want. Follow the other instructions. For extra fun, fold mini cookies into the giant one so you have cookies inside cookies. Or toss mini cookies with popcorn for the ultimate movie night snack.

So Cheesy

Now that you've conquered the kitchen, it's time to get busy! Start with these simple cheese straws. Then tackle the rest of the recipes until you're a master chef!

- ½ cup (120 milliliters) grated Parmesan cheese
- cutting board
- 1 package puff pastry
- 2 teaspoons (10 mL) Italian seasoning
- rolling pin
- pizza cutter
- baking sheet

1. Pre-heat the oven to 375°F (190°C).

2. Sprinkle half the Parmesan cheese across the cutting board. Lay a puff pastry sheet over the cheese-sprinkled board.

3. Scatter Italian seasoning and the rest of the cheese over the top of the pastry sheet.

4. Use a rolling pin to roll the dough until it is around ⅛-inch (.3-centimeter) thick. Press lightly, to make sure the cheese sticks to the dough.

5. Use a pizza cutter to cut the dough into long strips. Twist each strip several times and place on a greased baking sheet. Bake the cheese strips until they turn crispy and golden.

Finding Your Flavor

These easy, cheesy sticks are totally customizable! Find your favorite flavor by trying some of these recipe ideas.

- Use another type of cheese, such as Swiss, Cheddar, or Gouda, instead of Parmesan.

- Use dried chives, parsley, rosemary, oregano, sage, or thyme instead of Italian seasoning. Or try taco seasoning, curry powder, or cheese flavoring.

- Add sundried tomatoes, diced pepperoni or salami, or fresh minced garlic.

- Add sesame or poppy seeds, Cayenne pepper, sea salt, or garlic powder.

- Try sweet instead of savory. Sprinkle twists with cinnamon sugar, cocoa powder, or brown sugar and candied nuts.

Keep the Party Poppin'

Momentum is a big part of any party. It's important not to let it burn out too soon! Part of a hostess' job is to sustain the shindig and make sure guests have a great time right up until closing time. Luckily, there are a few secret tricks of the trade.

Plan your party layout ahead of time. Do you want use different rooms for different parts of the party? Keep everyone outside? Think about the flow of activities and how you want to spend the day, and use that to decide where to place the different party elements. Proper spacing is key. It's important to make sure people aren't too spread out or all crowding into one small area.

Don't be afraid to delegate! Enlist one of your more outgoing friends as a secret helper. She can help you keep the energy level up and the conversation lively. She can also keep an eye out for people who might need a social pick-me-up. Ask another friend if they'll play "waiter." Having someone else worry about dirty dishes will be one less thing on your plate.

Choose your party times carefully. If it starts too early or ends too late, your guests may decide to show up later or leave early. And consider how long you want your party to be. Two to three hours is a good starting point. If you want your guests to stick around longer, plan things to fill the time. Movie nights or sleepovers are great ways to keep the party going into the wee hours.

Unless photo ops are part of your party theme, ask people to turn off their phones. Keep them focused on what's happening right now.

Introduce your guests as they arrive. Get the conversation flowing right away to help guests mingle. Try some of these icebreakers to get guests chatting.

If your life was a TV show, which one would it be? Sitcom or drama?

If someone's underwear was showing, would you say something?

Would you rather be super smart or super popular?

Would you rather be the worst player on the best team, or the best player on the worst team?

If your life had a theme song, what would it be?

If you could invite any three people over for dinner, who would you ask?

Would you rather time travel to the past or the future?

If you could be any famous person, who would you be?

Party Pom-Poms

Draw your guests' eyes with these pretty-in-pink pom-poms. They'll add a colorful touch to unused space in your party room.

- one package (8 to 10 sheets) tissue paper
- fishing line
- scissors

1. Spread out tissue paper. Leave the paper in a stack.

2. Fold the tissue paper accordion-style. Fold the same direction as the original fold lines. Continue until the whole piece is folded into a strip.

3. Tie a loop of fishing line around the center of the tissue paper strip.

4. Cut the ends of the tissue paper in a curved shape. You can also cut them like an arrow.

5. Hold the tissue strip in the center. Fan one side of the tissue paper.

6. Gently pull the individual sheets of tissue paper apart, toward the middle of the paper. Alternate sides so your pom-pom is even.

7. Repeat on the other side. Fluff the pom-pom, as needed.

8. Tie a long piece of fishing line to the original loop. Use the long piece to hang your pom-pom.

Optional: Layer different shades of tissue paper to create an ombre effect. For example, for pink ombre you could use dark pink, light pink, and white.

Dip the tips of the tissue paper strip into colored water. Let them soak for a few minutes. Allow them to dry completely before fluffing.

Pretty Poms

There are many ways to display your pretty pom-poms.

- Hang pom-poms at varying heights over your tablescape. Use a single color for a subtle effect. Mix up shades and colors for a more dramatic look.

- For a prettier presentation, hang pom-poms with ribbon or thin strips of tulle.

- Pile pom-poms together for a large and fluffy centerpiece.

- Glue mini pom-poms to toothpicks for fun cupcake toppers.

- Bunch pom-poms together to create a chandelier. Add Chinese lanterns or balloons in contrasting colors for extra flair.

- Make pom-poms of various sizes. String them vertically, from largest to smallest.

Light-Up Lantern

Light up your home movie theater with a string of origami lights. Find out how to fold your way to funky handmade décor.

- 6-inch (15-cm) square origami paper
- string of Christmas lights

1. Begin with the paper colored side up. Fold the paper in half in both directions, then unfold. Turn the paper over.

2. Fold the paper from corner to corner in both directions, then unfold.

3. Use the existing creases to pull the sides of the paper toward the center. Allow the paper to collapse into a triangle.

4. Fold the bottom corners of the top layer to the point. Repeat these folds on the back side of the model.

5. Fold the corners of the top layer to the center. Repeat behind.

6. Fold the tips of the top layer down to the center triangles. Repeat behind.

7. Tuck the two small triangles into the pocket of the center triangles. Repeat behind.

8. Spread the layers of the model apart slightly. Blow gently into the bottom hole to form a cube. Shape the cube's sides with fingers as needed.

9. Carefully insert a bulb from the string of lights into the hole.

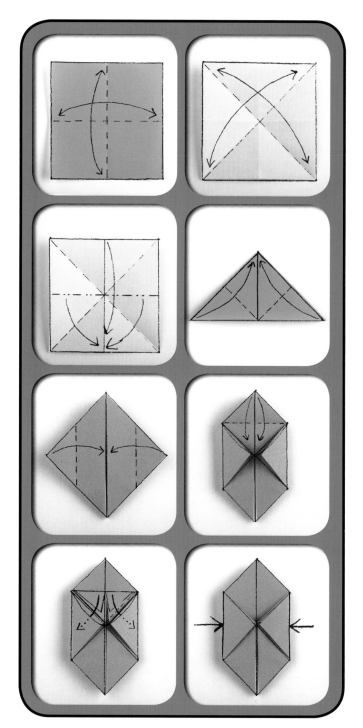

Origami Wisdom: Always press down firmly so that the creases are nice and crisp! Firm folding is a big part of origami success.

The Usual Suspects

No matter how much you prepare for your party, you can't control your guests' personalities. Meet the "usual suspects." Learn how to take on the party peeps who pose a special challenge for the hostess with the mostest. Figuring out your friends will make future party planning seem like a breeze!

"THE COMPLAINER:"

Nothing is ever quite good enough for this hard-to-please friend. The food is too cold. The music is too loud. The games aren't to her liking. She'll be sure to point out the problem to anyone who cares to listen.

HOW TO DEAL:

Some things are simply out of your control. Explain to the complainer that you're all there to have fun. Why let a little rain or a burnt pizza stop your good time? Your bright attitude just might be contagious.

"THE CHATTY KATHY:"

Good old Kathy. She loves to talk and never stops. Once she has your ear, it's hard for her to let go!

HOW TO DEAL:

Put the brakes on this runaway train by putting on your hostess hat. Excusing yourself to refresh the beverages or help out in the kitchen is a subtle yet effective way to escape.

"THE WALLFLOWER:"

The party is in full swing, but one of your guests looks like she'd rather be anywhere else. If you spot someone keeping to herself and not joining in, she just might be a wallflower.

HOW TO DEAL:

Not everyone wants to be the life of the party. As the hostess, it's your job to help everyone feel at ease. Make an effort to include the wallflower in your conversation, and steer it toward something you know she likes. Watch her light up when she talks about it.

Read More

Biddle, Steve. *Make Your Own Greeting Cards.* Mineola, N.Y.: Dover Publications, Inc., 2013.

Stephens, Sara Hines. *Do It Now! Crafts: Cool Art Projects & Tasty Snacks.* San Francisco: Weldon Owen Inc., 2012.

Wagner, Lisa. *Cool Game Day Parties: Beyond the Basics for Kids Who Cook.* Cool Young Chefs. Minneapolis: ABDO Publishing Company, 2014.

Internet Sites

FactHound offers a safe, fun way to find Internet sites related to this book. All of the sites on FactHound have been researched by our staff.

Here's all you do:

Visit *www.facthound.com*

Type in this code: 9781476540061

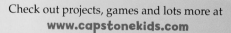
Check out projects, games and lots more at
www.capstonekids.com